PATTERFLASH

ACKNOWLEDGEMENTS

"From Huracan to Hardwood", staged as part of Leeds Transform, West Yorkshire Playhouse (2013), and originally published as a poem in *Any Change? Poetry in a Hostile Environment*, edited by Ian Duhig (Forward Arts Foundation, 2019)

"Tracy Emin", originally published in *Precocious* (Fruit Bruise Press/ Dog Horn Publishing, 2012)

"Easy Names", originally published in *Black and Gay in the UK*, edited by John R. Gordon & Rikki Beadle-Blair (Team Angelica, 2014)

"Kingdom of Us", originally published in a different form in *Clutching at Seashells* (Fruit Bruise Press/Dog Horn Publishing, 2009)

"Traces of Invasion", originally published in *Precocious* (Fruit Bruise Press/Dog Horn Publishing, 2012)

"Tryst with the Devil", originally published in *Ten: The New Wave*, edited by Karen McCarthy Woolf (Bloodaxe, 2014)

"Afterlife @ Aftershock", originally published in *Ten: The New Wave*, edited by Karen McCarthy Woolf (Bloodaxe, 2014)

"Boy-Machine", originally published in *Filigree: Contemporary Black British Poetry*, edited by Nii Ayikwei Parkes (Peepal Tree Press, 2018)

"Buzzing Affy", originally published in *Ten: The New Wave*, edited by Karen McCarthy Woolf (Bloodaxe, 2014)

"Mary", originally published in *Precocious* (Fruit Bruise Press/Dog Horn Publishing, 2012) and performed live by the BBC Players, with arrangement by Nikki Franklin

"The Kiss", originally published simultaneously in *Vada Magazine* (Dog Horn Publishing, 2014) and *Ten: The New Wave*, edited by Karen McCarthy Woolf (Bloodaxe, 2014)

"The Ways Might Love You, Given the Chance", originally published in *Precocious* (Fruit Bruise Press/Dog Horn Publishing, 2012)

"For Michael Sundin", originally published by LGBT+ History Month (Schools OUT UK, 2023)

ADAM LOWE

PATTERFLASH

PEEPAL TREE

First published in Great Britain in 2023
Peepal Tree Press Ltd
17 King's Avenue
Leeds LS6 1QS
UK

ISBN: 9781845235598

Printed in the United Kingdom
by Severn, Gloucester,
on responsibly sourced paper

MIX
Paper from
responsible sources
FSC
www.fsc.org   FSC® C022174

Supported by
ARTS COUNCIL
ENGLAND

CONTENTS

PRAISESONG OF BEDSIDE FANBOYS
BEFORE I WAS EVEN BORN

I can remember the day I was born,
don't you? There were meteor showers,
stars that went supernova in salute.

I can remember the rapturous applause,
outside my mum's hospital room.
She had to send them all home.

I remember the way the nurse held me up,
then slapped the other babies for not being
me. Don't you see? I was born to be a star.

I was to fill the hole in the sky where those
suns had blown up before. I was to shine
brighter than their rays could from a million miles.

All of this is true, I can assure you. My mum told
me so, and my dad confirmed it. I remember
the world stopped for me. Did it stop for you too?

THE POETS COULD FLY

i.

Mum used to tell us we were the most beautiful babies in the whole
wide world. Every mother believes it, but no one believed it like
my mum. She could tell you you were starlight and truth with enough
conviction it became so. That was the power she had.

Inside us, there would always be that voice of hers which,
if we listened to it, would convince us of whatever
we needed to hear. She would tell us, even from afar,
of the right choice to make justice happen.

So we did. I can hear her now and feel the joy of her embrace,
and hear the way she sang 'Barbara Allen' and 'My Bonnie Lies
Over the Ocean', the way her mother never did for her.
And whatever else, of this we can be sure.

ii.

The feeling that swept up, ready and raw on blonde crests,
was new to me but felt ancient. It must have been sitting there
waiting for a time like this to emerge.

Seeing those beautiful black faces reflected, welcoming,
made me lighter than I thought I had the right to be.
Fit to burst, I was ready. I was provoked and willing to sit

in the discomfort of who I was and who I had been and who
I should yet be. I would do this. I would be this. I'd take a moment
to breathe and hold it in. I would fill with it, ready

to smile, to sigh and to shake. Soon, I'd be flying,
and we'd hold hands in an arc over the horizon,
black bodies threaded like beads, together against the sun.

iii.

It's hard to say one deserves anything.
In truth, luck and birthright
play more of a part.
But I am happy to feel that I am here.
As much as I can, I have worked.
As much as I can, I have cleared the path.

MAROON IN BLONDE

At four years old I decided I would have blonde hair.
Then I could be Princess Aurora from *Sleeping Beauty*.

Dad and I were in the market for wigs.
Dad cast bright in ginger; me, maroon.

In Chapeltown they called him Redbeard.
I didn't have a nickname, yet. (Beyonce would come later.)

We couldn't have been more different.
When we ventured outside Chapeltown,

we would get *the look*.
Curiosity mixed with suspicion.

Was he my father, or was he some unkempt,
denim-loving older gent with Vaseline in his back pocket?

I wanted blonde hair not because
I wanted to look more like Dad

but because I knew that if I dressed up
like a princess or a diva, I would have a story worth telling.

We were hunting through jungles of fibre-optic lamps,
acrylic nails, gravy-drenched Yorkshire puddings.

The hair shops were always crowded with West Indian women
checking out weaves and lace fronts.

Armed with curling tongs and straighteners.
they debated the Desi girls about the virtues

of Empire skin bleaching cream,
and how far they would go to be 'British beautiful'.

But I just saw the shimmering pelts.
Those glorious wigs. I strode towards them.

The wigs had been waiting.
Blonde curls. Brunette bangs. Red rings.

Each wig a queer chrysalis.
They would lend me their wings.

They would give me their height,
they would give me their song.

Then I saw it: bold in gold, an angel's nimbus,
backlit by the strips. I said, 'Father,

you had best buy your child that exquisite wig!'
(Or perhaps words more appropriate to a four-year-old.

But he got the gist.) Between the nylon shine
and the transformation that overcame me,

my feet took flight and I danced.
I was still dancing when Dad took me to the pub

like a balloon of spun sunlight
on the last thread of reality.

The rest of the afternoon, I showered
his drinking buddies in a glitter of stories.

None quite came out right. A wooden Red Riding Hood
ate a magic apple and fell asleep.

When the wicked queen put a glass slipper
back on Red's foot, she woke up a real girl.

She and the queen turned the prince into a merman,
before they tossed him and his bride back into the sea.

I guess I knew the real stories.
I just preferred them my own way.

THE QUEEN'S SHILLING

To receive the Queen's Shilling, my grandma,
Margaret Kay Thorp – preggers, skint, and kicked
out of family home – coined herself a cunning stunt.
She headed down to t'Army, with Mary Frame
to sign up for the dosh. Their plan: to join now and claim
the meagre wins to feed them, her conny coat hiding
the young'un who slowly ripened inside. After,
they sauntered to the pub, to rejoice in the cleverness
of their crooked plot. When, at last, they'd be called to duty,
Nana'd be bursting upfront, and Mary back in Scotland,
both unable to serve. The brass wouldn't dare challenge
these Seacroft lasses, armed with heavy handbags, who
couldn't stop a pig in an alleyway but who could stop men
in suits with nary a look. So Nana, working class hero, pulled off
her plan to keep the Queen's Shilling without serving a day.

THE DOOR HANDLE

For Lisa and Andrea Dunbar. RIP.

Locked in the bedroom without a handle, all spoons and
knives taken so we couldn't open the door, we kindled

a fire from the mattress. We were young, just being mad kids,
burning paper, and the next thing we knew we were trapped.

We beat on the glass, against the window, calling for anyone
passing by on The Arbor to hear us. The smoke snaked

up to the ceiling, an upside-down fountain of grey ghosts,
our little lungs chugged on the gauzy air. Mum only

let us out when she was dressed back then. On a morning,
when she was good and ready. We were locked in our prison.

It was my fault, I think, this time. We weren't supposed to be
locked in but the handle had come off again. And Lorraine

was burning pretty patterns into paper with the matches
when we realised our mistake. Mum should've known better

after what she went through. She should've taken better care of us,
instead of treating us like her own parents treated her.

We were actors reading the same script. You'd never know it,
but we did want to love this place. These streets. Even when we left,

our hearts stayed, chasing each other in circles. Mum died first,
falling in the Beacon on Reevy Road. Then Lorraine got sent down.

In the end I was swept up, too, into that memory of Buttershaw
where it never rains, and dogs always play on the green in the sun.

A GLOSSARY OF POLARI

Affaire – a lover, a serious partner; someone you've had more than thrice.

Ajax – adjacent, beside; where you hope your affaire might be.

'arry varry (Harry varry) – arrive (backformation from Italian: arrivare); the perfect time to make an entrance.

Aunt nell – ear, listen (also: nellyarda); something best pricked to all the patter flash.

Auntie – older gay man, role model; sadly, not the Beeb (see "For Michael Sundin")

Back slum – public lavatory; somewhere to get your rocks off, natch.

Becker – wind (from Romani); the kind that spoils your hair, not the kind that stinks the room out.

Bona – good; that quality which is shared by Whitney, Cher, Madonna, etc.

The bones – a boyfriend or husband; perhaps an *affaire* if you've shagged him more than a dozen times.

Brandy – bottom (from Cockney rhyming slang: 'brandy and rum'); something a gay man might tip instead of velvet (if you catch my drift).

Brandy latch – toilet; something you probably want to lock shut while you have your mouth full.

Brown bread – dead; sometimes the result of gagging too hard.

Cap – head; the body part, not the act.

Charpering – finding; made much easier with Grindr.

Charpering carsey – police cell; somewhere many entrapped men wound up.

Cheuri – tongue, speech; a vicious weapon in the right hands.

Chidder – wonder (backformation from Italian: chiedersi); what Alice felt on her adventures.

Dolly – pretty; not a reference to the diva Parton, but it seems fitting anyway.

Eek, ecaf – face (from backslang); the thing's that irrelevant in a dark room.

Fairy – soul or spirit; if capitalised, She, the Holy Spirit Herself.

Gardy loo – 'Look out!' Too late. You're covered in piss again (see also: 'Connoisseur in a Fetish Club).

Grinzer – wrinkle (backformation from Italian: grinza); something I don't get because *Black don't crack*, sweetie. Etc, etc. Blah blah blah.

Grop – knot; something you'll learn to make an untie at the Scouts, which you can finally join openly now, by the way.

Harva – anal sex; the full-a not the half-a.

Head – bed; the place where you might also give some…

Hoof – dance; trot out like a prize pony, darling, and shake your tassles.

Ink – stink, smell (from Cockney rhyming slang: pen and ink); the odour of bullshit at an inopportune moment.

Jin – door; not the drink, but I'll have one as soon as I walk through this.

Jinny, jinnik – to know; probably not in the Biblical sense, but language is elastic…

Journo – day; not a journalist, in this context.

Lallies – legs; you've got a great pair!

Laus – chases; give this up.

Lills – hands; Madonna's are legendary.

Mama – mentor, drag mother, an elder queen; what I might be in a hundred years.

Meat rack – brothel; not a viable career option long-term.

Mumper – candle (from Romani); something you shouldn't bring to a dark room gathering.

Munge – darkness; the best thing about said dark room gathering.

Nochy – night; when all the vamps and queers come out to play.

Ochy – look (backformation from Italian: occhiata); not quite as sumptuous as vada.

Omi – man; I'll have three, please.

Oven – mouth; not for buns.

Pagament – satisfaction (backformation from Italian: appagamento); a Benni Benassi song.

Patter flash – gossip, chat, ostentatious or pretentious speech; the lyrics pouring out my gob.

Pogey – money; it's uncouth to talk about it.

Pooker – to speak or ask (from Romani: 'pooker', which means Romani slang itself); something I'm fond of doing.

Randall – candle (from Cockney rhyming slang: Harry Randall); best kept away from hair spray (but also, see above).

Reef – to feel, to grope (especially the bulge or crotch); frowned upon when you don't have permission.

Sally – rise, ascend, lift (backformation from Italian: salire); the name of every single faghag you've ever met. Love ya babes.

Scotches – legs; maybe because there are usually good ones under kilts?

Sharda – though; maybe a fabulous drag name.

Shroud – cloud (from Cockney rhyming slang: Turin shroud); the cover of which is ideal for escaping sunlight's harsh glare when hungover.

Sindarry – to light, kindle, switch on (backformation from Italian: 'accendare'); perhaps something you'd do when your sex life is dead.

soap – dope (from Cockney rhyming slang: Joe Soap); sometimes paired with beauty, as in a himbo.

Squash – wash (from Cockney rhyming slang: Bob Squash); what you should do if you ignored my gardy loo.

The Dilly – Piccadilly (in London or Manchester), a high street or similar; the rebar above the Village.

Thews – thighs, sinews; something to lick.

Trade – a sexual partner; only sometimes a prostitute's 'john'; once the name of a famous club.

Trick – a sexual partner; nearly always a prostitute's 'john'; maybe so called because you rely on hiding your face in the dark to pull one.

Troll – walk, provoke (as in online); often done under the bridge when cruising, aptly enough.

Vada – see, spy, look; sounds like Prada.

Vast – covered; what you want to do to your willy if in bed with a stranger.

Venny – come out; what Shirley Bassey sang about thanks to Pink!

Vera – gin (from Cockney rhyming slang: Vera Lynne); with slimline, please!

Vochy – voice, speak; mine's gone like Ariel's after a night on the town with the Sea Witch.

Yews – eyes; what you vada the thews with, soap.

Zitarry – mention; what people do when they '@' you on Twitter.

DOWNLOW DOWNLOAD

Age: barely legal. Sex: on demand.
Location: inside you. What are you
wearing? Nothing – a mask.
A thousand pics of the perfect dick.
Come: my virtual world. Slip in
greasy digits. Breathe heavy
across the wires. Anonymous
lovers from Fitlads, Gaydar, Scruff.
Search cock size, skin tone, clique.
Click. Push enter. Sticky keys under
salt fingers poke boys across continents
at supersonic speed. I like you. Search
wavelengths to find you; download your bits.
Unencrypted – viral load for twenty quid.

ELEGY FOR THE LATTER-DAY TEEN WILDERNESS YEARS

Joan, Trashley and Gingerella lived in a one-bed flat. You'd never seen gurrls
with more poise. Our style made them sick. We had a cribbed language

others didn't understand and that gave us power. We made the streetlights
our spots. We were fierce, *En Vogue*. We spoke in the high tones

of the grand dames, sashayed and preened. There we were royalty.
You should've seen that long coat drag along the floor. We found the fake fur

in a skip but wore it like mink. We were kings, rooting in bins
round the back of Queens Court, living thrifty and spare.

We would hold hands and link arms on the march to some nearby-far
        after party.
We could leap across the horizon in electric blue heels and banish bigots
        with a look.

In dim chillouts, we made community with chatter and gossip, hugs
that bookended us on the couch and on the bed. Ours was a world

where our love for each other went unsaid, expressed in nicknames
and twisting hips. I was Beyonce, you were Mariah, she was Violette.

We lived in the witching, hybrid hours, where the dark and dim had
        pride of place.
We were bold and wild, our songs ricocheted against the naked heavens.

Then the clouds would thicken like stones, and we'd retreat; the morning
pouring over us like molten gold, swallowing the glitter and bruises of night.

GINGERELLA'S DATE

Girl, I only agreed because I was starvin' and sick of plain pasta.
        Not even tomatah!
I wo' dead skint, so I suggested we go fer a curry in Wigan. I thought
        it would scare 'im off.

I hoped I'd have bad breath to keep him away. But anyway, he wo'n't
        havin' it.
He wanted me. So I played along. Ordered mixed starter
        with giant fuck-off king prawns,

lamb chops, samosas, the lot. Then I 'ad a butter chicken masala,
        and yer know I'm lactose intolerant!
Had that with garlic naan an' some pilau an' all. Then washed it down
        with a jug of mango lassi

and a bottle of rosé. I told the most filthy and obnoxious jokes.
        He lapped it up, didn't he!
Dirty ol' git woulda gone wi' me whatever I said. So I thought, fuck it!
        In for a penny, in for a pound!

I wo' outrageous, Bey! I ordered some kulfi ice cream too.
        Me gut wo' proper churning.
It wo' like a washing machine full of shit,
        you know what I mean?

Proper agony, right, but girl, it wo' proper good grub! I'd do it again
        right now if yer offered it me.
You know the curries where they just have that dirty grease
        in little puddles on the top?

Fuckin' fit, I tell yer! I ate the piggin' lot. And to top it all off,
        I had an Americano, just to make sure
I tasted proper rank. Then when the bill came, he looked so pleased.
        Slapped down twenny pound notes

like he wo' the Big I Am, right. But I could see what 'e wo' plannin'
      to do to my *lily white ass*,
and I tell yer now, Tanya Turner might be a slapper, but I
      ain't desperate, girl!

So I asked him to go get me some fags from the shop over't road
      before we left. Said I needed the loo, like,
you know. But when the man came to collect the money, I asked
      him for a doggy-bag

and told him to be quick. They got me all them leftovers wrapped up
      in less than two minutes.
I swear, they're proper geniuses down at Akbar's. And then,
      before 'e got back, I legged it, bags in 'and.

Only, he saw me, didn't he? Yelled after me like, 'Oi! Where
      you fink you're off to?'
So I just waved him a pair of Vs and kept runnin'. I'll tell you
      what, though:

I need to stop smokin'. It fuckin' killed me runnin' up that hill.
      But it wo' worth it for that curry.
Worth it not to have to have plain spaghetti yet again. As I always say,
      A girl's gotta eat!

VADA THAT

Aunt nell the patter flash and gardy loo!
Bijou, she trolls, bold, on lallies
slick as stripes down the Dilly.

She minces past the brandy latch
to vada dolly dish for trade, silly
with oomph and taste to park.

She'll reef you on her vagaries –
should you be so lucky. She plans
to gam a steamer and tip the brandy,

but give her starters and she'll be happy
to give up for the harva. Mais oui,
she's got your number, duckie.

She'll cruise an omi with fabulosa bod,
regard the scotches, the thews, the rod –
charpering a carsey for the trick.

Slick, she bamboozles the ogles
of old Lilly Law. She swishes
through town, 'alf meshigener, and blows

lamors through the oxy at all
the passing trade. She'll sass a drink
of aqua da vida, wallop with vera in claw.

Nellyarda her voche's chant till the nochy
with panache becomes journo, till
the sparkle laus the munge out of guard.

But sharda she's got nada, she aches
for an affaire, and dreams of pogey
through years of nix. The game nanti works

— not for her. She prefers a head
or back slum to the meat rack. Fact is,
she'll end up in the charpering carsey

of Jennifer Justice. What is this
queer ken she's in? Give her an auntie
or a mama. The bones isn't needed just yet.

Though she's a bimbo bit of hard,
she's royal and tart. And girl, you know
vadaing her eek is always bona.

FUCKING

after Dorianne Laux's 'Kissing'

They are fucking in park bushes,
revolting against beds or families,
sometimes by the roadside
in a purring Jeep Sport.

Fucking as urinals brim unused;
the cubicles overcrowded,
pierced through with a simple hole
that winks pink to welcome you.

Fucking in the daylight, high noon,
uncaring of propriety – because
they can be, because at times
it's all that can be done.

Fucking spread like the Lord
on the Cross, kissed by Judas,
thorn-torn, getting nailed, as
a terrier sniffs them out in the dust.

SHE'S ON THE CHING AGAIN

To all the late-night dancers at the Thompson Arms

She's on the Ching again, babe,
buzzing alone on the dancefloor
where she loves us all like family.

Sweat glittering like tinsel,
she's Sylvester, a mirrorball,
in her own little world.

She's Scouse-soused tonight,
her voice electric blue flight,
her eyes twinklin' stars of dew in the limelight.

Energised on gossip,
her bald head's a piston,
her gob, a serenade that echoes under rigging.

Lavender and golden,
we've all gotta wind it,
all gotta be her tonight; she has spoken.

With stories to regale yer;
with 'er hands, she's conductor;
and she's vibin' to feel yer, yer feel me? Yer feel her.

ELSIE TANNER FOR TEENS

with thanks to Caleb Everett

I pull a poet on a Sunday night. His flamboyant word-love
a pretentious march of assonance, allusion, pop-culture
and puns as ghastly colourful as the scarf he found and flings
cheekily around his neck. We plan to escape the dullard dross,
the twosome hitting on us: one with a pulled-tight robot face,
the other a fleshy half-alien. They tell us they love us. Poet boy says
he wants romance like the notes harping in his blood; he wants
foggy departures on steam trains. Robot boy offers to walk him
to Piccadilly Station. I don't think he understands. Alien boy boasts
he's boring. We gleefully agree. I pull the poet on a Sunday night
to flee the clones, but because I also want to taste his words, hear
that magnificent, dragonish drag-voice sigh. His enjambments
shudder through me. We spoon through dawn like quotation marks
or double quavers. You see, he's Elsie Tanner for teens. On Monday,
he talks me silly. He has to leave. I vomit an alphabet of new meanings
and yearn to be silly again. I want us to sprout nonsense in sheaves.

MAGICIAN ON AISLE TWO

It's his Sunday afternoon party trick,
as he lifts golden bricks of Cathedral City
in the supermarket fluorescence and vanishes
them away with such sleight of hand
the security guard doesn't blink.

His second act is to place hands on Patak's sauce
like the glass on a ouija board and spell
out messages from dead celebrities like
Marx and Ché and Robin Hood: 'free',
'revolution', 'take from the rich', 'give to the poor'.

Rabbits disappear inside hats, and baguettes
are sawn in two to better fit under his cape.
He tiptoes through the alarms, confident
he could slither out of any handcuffs,
disappear in a puff of Golden Virginia smoke.

Then, when home, for his final feat
he breaks bread and opens tinned sardines,
fills glasses from a milk carton full of wine,
and feeds something like five thousand
cheering him on in the back garden.

THAT MARY'S CAR BONNET

as reworked by Adam Lowe

'As tha vada'd that Mary's car bonnet?
        Fit as fook an' no debate.
        I'd rim 'er aht on't first date.
She's a bit o' rough in Triga gear innit:

Stunnin' lallies an' bulgin' basket,
        Aris like a pair of apples
        Bobbin' in an 'andkie.
I'd wear 'er like an Adidas 'at at Ascot.

Well let's pop on Grindr tuh see if she's on it;
        'it 'er up for right now discretion.
        Check for 'er preferred position.
'Ey up, she's "masc4masc". Into foot worship.

Can I pull it off? In t'past I've done it!
        Woulda slipped on me trackies
        Popped on t'old trainers…
She's a bit o' nice but 'er head's got nowt in it.

But it's too much hard work just for a bit;
        One straight look from me,
        She'll know I'm a queen.
Nah. Life's too short for forcin' a fit.

SHE'S ON HER WAY

Girl, she loves a line, but she'll never give one back.
Snort a thin one, cos she'll have it fat.

She knows everyone – from DJ to bouncer –
and takes anything she doesn't have to pay for.

She's glam, I'll give her that.
She can blag a drink and sass the chat.

She's on her way, but she's not there yet.
Until then, she'll have yours, pet.

CONNOISSEUR IN A FETISH CLUB

In loving memory of Sly Hands, King of the Rubbermen

He strides over as I take a leak.
He reaches out a plastic cup
and catches my yellow streak.

With a wink and a nod, he toasts me,
and gulps down golden rain:
Mmm! Sweet homemade lemonade!

As I turn to get lost,
among the leather and vinyl,
among the bears and the dross,

I think: Next time, I should offer him
a champagne flute. Serve it sparkling
like Veuve Reserve 42, by the bottle

rather than the glass. And I would ask
if it quenches his thirst, or if he's testing me for diabetes.
But it's good to know there's value

even in piss, so casually discarded.
It's like water to sluicing wine:
in the right hands, it changes, become sublime.

SNAPPING THE STARS

Inspired by Alison Henry's photo 'Charlie, Provincetown 1996'

I never really knew Charlie – not well –
we just knew the same people.

We stumbled together through the same
summer string of hot after-parties,

occasionally hand in hand, or arm in arm,
in the manic dawn quest for a welcoming off-licence.

Charlie was ethereal. One of those skinny boys
with translucent hair slicked across his face,

girlish hands, girlish hips, and laughter
like a flock of lavender balloons.

I used to photograph hundreds of boys
just like Charlie. Boys where you could

see heaven through their skin. Boys
that danced down Old Compton Street.

Now I take snaps for magazines, it's these
beautiful young girls – cool girls that look

like the boys I knew. And when they laugh,
I think back, and I'd rather be like Charlie:

translucent, only seen at twilight, laughing
rubber bubbles of colour at the stars.

FRUIT

You call me a fruit,
and I agree,
say

a fruit is ripe,
promising seeds,
bursting with juice;

a fruit is rich,
remembers its roots,
makes a display of any table.

I say,
I am the apple
that announces the gravity

of a given situation;
the pomegranate
whose gemstones teach

the burden of possession;
the fig
our ancestors couldn't resist.

You call me a fruit
and I agree:
soft, round and sweet.

Peel back my layers,
take a look at my pips.
Full as a melon,

sharp as a lime,
come over here
and bite me.

JEZEBEL, GUILTY, QUEEN

You call me Jezebel: temptress, false idol
in shallow spotlight, pedlar of blasphemy and unnatural sex.

You call me guilty: unsuited, shock slut of back alleys,
siren seed-spilling in the thrashing of night.

You call me a queen. Paint me Anne Boleyn.
Paste on my make-up, sharp-set and glittering.

These pearls I clutch as sexy rosaries.
Before you silence me, know this:

though headless, I'll sing.
I'll go down in history.

BOUQUET AND BANQUET

Lead with your nose. Fresh-cut flowers. The salty cure of bacon frying on November mornings, beside sunny eggs dappled with grease, mushrooms turned grey, and the brown of caramelising onions that cut through cloudcover and the smell of damp leaves. Cod and haddock at war for your chippy. Malt vinegar. Vietnamese coffee with condensed milk, the sweet paradise from a tin, imbibed in glass cups, notes of cinnamon. Cardamom, ginger, paprika and thyme. That clean waft of tender flesh, game on game row, a rose-red smell of sinew and fat on hook and slab. Russian pancakes – origami serviettes clutching rice and spring onion, blinis with apple and syrup. Cocoa butter and olive oil upon Empired skin. Pasties to suit you: handmade, fluffy. Potato and meat, parcelled in Yorkshire pastry – hearty, homely – most definitely the food of Leodesian gods. Take it all in.

BEAUTY ON ROW 5

Eat her skin, washed clean with red rose water,
now smooth as Black Soap; rub the ointment in:
Fair & White, Paris, to cure her heart of darkness.
A massage of Clairissime Cosmetique Body Clear
Complexion Lotion; Red Fox Tub o' Butter for burned limbs;
Clear 'N' Smooth Swiss Collagen Cream to fill the holes.
She grows from Dax Virgin Hair Fertilizer. Regard jaguar blue
irises between maroon wreaths, contact lenses – look, hope.

Kiss those parted, fruiting lips, honeyed with paraffin
Vaseline Blue Seal. Smell the Royal Bees Waxed hair.
Crushed flat with GHDs, like queen of the night tulips
between pages under a bed leg. See the curves, airbrushed
by Dr James' Stretch Mark Cream, Dr James' Slimming
Body Scrub and Dr James' Hip Up and Buttock Gel. She
is Provate Lady White, an oil painting on mahogany;
she is made of acrylic, cocoa butter and kerosene.

THEY CAME IN TWO BY TWO

after Alexandra Lazar's 'Visceral Is an Animal' and
'Little Vegan Butch Girl Wins on Points'

As you raged
your mouth descended into a snout.

You screamed like a tapir,
ravaged slice-wounds into my skin;

as we tussled you bent me
like a rainbowed arch,

face against
the mat. Pinned there,

I felt you plough me
like an ox.

Your sinews glistened against my flanks.
You pawed me, tiger;

feasted
on the protests of my skin.

REYNARDINE FOR RED

You were Reynard, Fox King, red with cunning. I was on your tail.
I thought I was the hunter, but you led me deeper through
haunted woods. Though roots rose in treachery and thorns lay
snags along the path, I was quick, eager to find your

wooded palace. When the tangled boughs grew ragged
and the forest yawned, there I found it, yellow stone,
all battlements and iron doors. There was a special knock
to get inside. You showed me how to do it, as if I could still trust you,

even after you waylaid me. When the doors opened, I smelled
musk and filth, but your charm was enough to ignore it.
Inside, was like your love: labyrinthine, gnarly,
the dead ends cauterised nerves.

I grew more obsessed, a vixen bride.
The mirrors were twisted, threw up cracked reflections
of my form. I spun around myself.
Reynard, saw your teeth a gleaming knife in a pink maw.

You paw shirt buttons to expose my heart. You took all that
you wanted. You sank fangs into skin, lapped at the muscle, pulled
my fingernails from their beds. You threw me, hard, broke my bones,
my left eye corkscrewed from my face. You savaged

my nose, left it torn and bleeding. You smashed my fingers.
Grabbed by my hair, you pounded me into cruel stone.
You counted my teeth scattered on the floor. You tore my stomach
open, insides unravelled. This was how you preferred me.

But I refused to remain broken. I used spit and rheum
to glue my porcelain bones back together. I relied on rage to move
busted joints, to rise from the straw on the cell floor. Every hair
on my skin bristled, every strand a flame. Red Dog-man, I was ready

to come for you. I scooped up my shattered teeth and wedged them
into gums, my smile, a wounded cherry. I reset the twisted arm,
leaned backwards to unbend my spine. I pressed on the wrenched nails,
till they settled like glass tombstones. I popped

the eye in place, its sickening kiss robbing me of appetite.
I bundled my guts back in, tucked tail between my legs. Rage turned
to design. I planned my lure. You liked weakness.
You loved me best when I begged and pleaded.

I hauled my tortured self through endless turns until I found your bedchamber
and lay before the door. When the loneliness took you, in the hours
between night and morning, you came out and found me. I blubbered.
and I mewled. I cried. You took me into your bed. Snuggled

against me for warmth. We fucked, and I tore a tuft
of red hair. You liked it. You yawned, slimed with cum, then slept.
Sneaky, nocturnal, I slid out of place and fashioned a rope of sheets.
Opened the window. I dropped to ground.

I ran through the forest, leaving the hair like a trail of breadcrumbs.
Come morning, while you still slept, I returned with hunters and their dogs.
The beasts sniffed your scent, tasted the essence of fur in air.
We arrived at the castle. The special knock let us in.

The hounds followed your smell through the maze. When they came
upon your lair and began to tear you open, I yelped. They shredded
your coat, tore bone from breast, and I nuzzled in and chewed
your warm flesh. Then, there was nothing left of you, your blood lapped

from flagstones. For days afterward, I wandered your labyrinth,
freeing your victims from their cells. Most were pleased to follow.
Some, trapped so long, could not bear the light. At last, castle mine,
I watched to make sure as I burned it to the ground.

LATE NIGHT SHOPPING

You wait by the frozen turkeys,
covered in goosebumps. Through your
joggers I can see your icicle dick,
the shape of it. Long. I've got
my hand on frozen peas, an excuse
to be here at 3am. Just the noise
of shelf-stackers in the crisps aisle,
enough to cover the rustle as you slide
your hand down, revealing a bulge
in white Ginch Gonch. You pop it
out, creamy as a Mini Milk, and stroke
it gently, working forefinger and thumb
towards the tip. I don't move
but I watch, as you spill spunk
all over the cryo-sleep poultry.
I buy the peas, some milk,
and a Calippo, and checking
my palm, I feel short-changed.

BOTTLED UP, FOR THE HOUSEBOUND

He was trying to explain how the rain was different for him every time.
– he describing its danger, as I described grief.

Once it was warm on his tongue as pavements and sunshine.
Once it was cold, beads striking his skin, his recollection

so sharp against the dullness of my own, rounded where I was flat.
So he came to bring me the treasure of recollection, a wounded butterfly

scissoring in a child's hand. He told me it was smell that perplexed him most.
He laid a path through forests of memory. The stories broke me with envy.

In winter, he swore the rain smelled like smoke, until snow fell.
All I could smell was a plastic Christmas tree. By spring, it was fog on stone,

wet twigs, fresh moss, tree sap seeping, notes of ambergris, aldehydes,
maybe buds in their big push, and bacteria breathing bouquet beetroot.

March, he said, had the aroma of black bark. Thunder storms metallic
but humid. He left me these memories as I lay in bed and he flew off.

In an Old Delhi shop, he found an attar called Mitti and sent it with
the label, *For the memories*. It let me fly backward through seasons, traverse forests,

sit in healing downpour and watch rivers swell, even from the prison
    of my house.
Now I watch rain at my window, feel its weight, smell the soil, and whirl again.

CARRION FLIGHT OF THE HARPSICHORDS

With thanks to Ian Duhig

Son of Norman McCaig, anatomist,
Ewan builds harpsichords with vulture
quills to make his own kind of poetry,
when the bony keys are tapped like ribs.

Flemish-style virginals; open casket
muselars, ottavinos and spinets;
katabatic instruments assembled with passion,
hunger and flair. Compassed and pitched,

when played, they flew him on scavenger wings,
to soar rapterish above Gott's Park.

CEMETERY AT STIFT SANKT PETER, SALZBURG OLD TOWN

They didn't do things like us,
that full-of-colour, always
velvet, gilt with pride kind.

Their psychopomp ceremony makes
our dry ground blush, with
those wet mouths of yellow,

blue, violet flowers; the gothic
without irony; the emblems,
fallen stars fused into sunset

marble. If we'd celebrated
our dead with the same brazen
glory, the same palaces of praise,

we'd hold lavish portraits of them
in the lime catacombs of our hearts,
instead of tending cold slabs of stone.

THE CLIMB

In loving memory of Ben McNichol

The nurse left him happily eating noodles,
his grin an honest deception.

If he was quick, she'd never have time to stop him.
She'd be too busy checking on the others.

She noted his mood and general demeanour,
before she crossed him off her list.

With her gone, he shook the fabric
of the late-night memories sewn inside.

With a twist he made a serpent,
and wrung the sheets with balled fists.

In his hands he felt power and knowledge.
He would know what nothing was.

He wanted to be forgotten,
but mostly to forget:

that circle of men, the compensation,
the price paid in his flesh.

It was a way to escape their clutches
after all these years inside him.

He threaded the snake around his throat,
for a second a feather boa.

Then he bound one end to the window latch,
and leant back to test its strength.

He spread his arms wide in glory,
preparing for the final act.

He took a moment to study his game,
looked down at his imaginary crowd.

They could see him now,
weight poised on wire,

ready for this high-dive.
He stepped out, pleased

there was no one there
to intervene or catch him.

And at last he fell, one graceful plunge,
and was freed as gravity snapped him.

HARRY, TIME-TRAVELLER

for Harry Nihill, Hulme History Society

They move through his memory like record keepers. He, the
guardian of ancient texts; a librarian of lost histories. Blinked out of
existence, now it's apocrypha in language that won't translate.

This knowledge he knows can't be passed on as easily as last breaths.
Alexandria. Constantinople. Nishapur. All dead. His archive under
siege, blitzed by tirade of age, pulled down, brick by elegiac brick;

community that fails to retain. Regret creeps, oily, languid, between
syllables, but as he speaks, we young things enrapt, a movement
begins, at last. After all these years, the time-traveller journeys back.

BONE RAILROAD

I will clutch your bones together
into a coral palace at the bottom
of the sea. I will sing hymns

to celebrate you in the vault
built from your ribcages. The stained
glass I will blow from your dreams.

Who cast you down here like
a bone railroad from Africa's west
coast to the Americas, the Caribbean?

Whales will worship you.
I will come down and sit upon
your coral throne, and remember

who you were. I will unearth
your stories, find the ships that
discarded you, and sink them all.

FOR MICHAEL SUNDIN

You wheel around the garden with Elton,
dragons guarding the neatly striped grass.

You splash in his pool, while Sir Elt rides
his exercise bike, festooned at neck and shoulders

with bananas. Michael, forget the tabloids and Auntie.
They didn't appreciate your grace and good nature.

Spinning like a sirocco – even beside Elton you're too bold
for TV. With the bear cub in hand you look like

someone I once knew and loved. You could be any of us –
a literal friend of Dorothy. Immortalised in shorts,

standing in the bottom half of Tik-Tok, the Great Army of Oz;
or talking all things over the rainbow in yellow slacks

and a snowman jumper on Blue Peter. Michael,
your Northeastern accent, that gap between your teeth –

you are darling. How you leap over their prejudices,
a delight even as you water the tortoise on screen.

I weep to see those photos of you smiling, knowing
what's behind those eyes. You're moving Technicolor;

their world's still in black and white. Celluloid can't hold you back.
You're too big for their broom cupboard; too true to lie.

MONUMENT FOR THE FALLEN IN INK AND PAPER, 2020

Sophia Mirza. Merryn Crofts. Bob.
The monument we have for you

stands in the sky of our memories,
casting its long shadow over

the horizon we stand upon now
as free and heard and living.

We stand as memorial, polished stone
and hushed voices. Our phalanx waves

your names as our standard.
And know this: you kept us going,

were the flame that gasped steam
that moved the machine of the wheel

which is at last turning. You were
the lives we lost, sacred, ours,

in that footfall onward to victory.
We stand on the farther shore

and smile back only because of you.
We cannot revive you. But we can

restore you with love and in
the sweetness of what we have

achieved. When next we meet,
there will be rejoicing.

THE SIGHT OF A SYRIAN BOY RECLINING ON YOUTUBE

In memory of Hamza al-Khateeb. RIP.

Bathed by his loved ones, adorned in white roses,
he defers soil and in public reposes.
Reclined, he stands tall, brave against injustice.

His body describes the shape of corruption.
Black craters bloomed where bullets tore him open.
But look, even now, he has skies in his skin.

Thirteen and broken, flesh burned by cigarettes.
He was tortured, kneecapped, after his arrest
emasculated in the march for progress.

Look at him; he watched pigeons in the morning.
See the snapped neck beneath his puppy-fat chin.
His name is a storm, gathered and rumbling.

Look how they lie and claim there's no evidence,
that there's no sign at all of such brute violence.
But look, see the bruises turned blue on his face.

Washed by his loved ones, adorned in pale roses,
he awaits soil and in public reposes.
Reclined, he still stands, brave against injustice.

TRACY EMIN

after David Tait's 'Nadav Kander'

I lie in state above our covers and hit your voicemail.
I want to talk about Tracy Emin as I read the sheets.

I imagine we're riding her bed. It's a sordid flying
carpet dragged down the effluent of the Thames.

We leave a greasy smear on the surface,
and sail through clouds of purple smoke.

I'm mortified, unable to enjoy Tower Bridge,
its iron speckled dried blood orange.

I'm glad for the beep and the silence
that follows. I haven't paid your bill.

I'll imagine I'm the cigarettes, you're the ash.
I'll lie a while longer. This call can wait.

EASY NAMES

Down at the craft centre, after our fucking was done, we attempted to make jewellery. But he said he wanted me to stay inside him. Wanted me to run beads in circuits round his balls. Wanted me to thread him with my mouth.

So we pulled string through rows of little glass gems and pretended it was us still fucking. Laid out, darting through, bunching ourselves together. The segments of a bracelet.

He slid into it, showing it off like a dowry. He wore the necklace I made like my spunk around his clavicle. He made a ring of the beads too, and wore that like my sphincter, tight against his knuckles.

When we returned home, we emptied and filled each other. We were the snake eating its own tail.

Afterwards, we lay around, deflated. The room still stank of sex. We looked at the jewellery we had made. It was cheap plastic. But pretty enough in its own way.

TOOTHBRUSH

You gulp down the last of the orange,
full of an advertisement's sunshine.
I follow as you climb the white stairs
barefoot, head angled against stars
spangled through the cocked skylight.
The bathroom fan whooshes muted
applause you break with the click
of a flipped toothpaste lid. You talk
about your new boyfriend as the room
shimmers around us. When you go to bed
I stare at the comets sliding towards
the plughole and their orange pulp flecks.
I clutch the basin for support and, before
bed, I push our toothbrushes together.

KINGDOM OF US

In barefoot horseplay we patter, conquer wet tombolos
turned castles. We sing ditties half-remembered
from childhood seaside outings. You frogleap over

my crooked back, legs slicked with brine. I finger through
limpid pools for surer answers, against the whispers of tide.
Hooves bellow, donkeys bray, seagulls laugh in the distance.

Your aftershave carries across the waves: a sirensong to expansion.
We claim structures built by others. I spin candy floss into jelly fish,
weave a kingdom of fine water-things. We build empires of dreams,

colonise half the beach but our trenches are invaded by unexpected
water creeping from beneath. The turrets dissolve, towers collapse,
walls become history. Newly dug holes swirl with ocean, start

swallowing toes, beg for better standing. Our day's firm footing
becomes seabed again. As surf rolls in, kingdoms swirl away,
made of nothing enduring. The foundations betray us to the sea.

TRACES OF INVASION

I start with your sock drawer,
looking for clues. He's not in the bathroom
where the usual signs should be found:
toothbrush, aftershave, maybe a razor
or spare inhaler. Neither is he in your
kitchen, a metaphor in spoons or knives,
rustling when one of us hungers. Nor
is he in the lounge, in the favourite pre-set
TV channels, the choice of furniture, or
the lived-in smell of your home.

So he must be in your bedroom,
hiding from one day to the next,
between the mattress and bed, or
under your wardrobe. But he's left
none of his clothes – tidy, unlike me,
who could never be clean enough to be
discrete. I find him eventually, misplaced
among bathrobes and towels where
a polaroid falls like it was buried
treasure, pressed between His and His.

AVALANCHE

i.

Manchester became an ice bowl that year.
White bluster hurried in knee-deep cascades

through Piccadilly basin. Ducks turned chilly
taxidermists' specimens as the canal seized up.

Telegraph wires became chandeliers
of ice. Trees became rigid charcoal spinsters,

and the ash-black road-top covered itself up.
Arctic velvet lined the tarmac. Traffic stopped.

ii.

We ran through the snow
before your tears could harden:

half-giggling, half-sobbing.
She had died, you'd said,

but she'd left you the speed.
So we tangoed in the snowfall

and galloped down Whitworth Street.
We threw ourselves together

like igloo bricks. We kissed, high
as snow crystals between the icing of stars.

We drew our names in the caster on cars.
I lost my house key, so we broke in,

flurried forward, piled by the door.
We buried there in duvets for warmth.

iii.

We were in love that night.
We were lying together.

Let's do this again, we said,
but we meant never.

TRYST WITH THE DEVIL

Come. Let me show you dewy wonders
here in the grass. Let me feel the flicker
of your tongue in my arse. Come

slide over me, muscular river,
rockstar-pornstar in the shape of an asp.
Splash your coat of stars across me,

wrap me in your night. Prophet
of rebels, let me taste your dissent;
wet me with your meteorites; with tongue

I'll trace your proud descent. King of things
that scrabble in the dirt, raise
your fallen army – drive it through me.

THE DAY TRUMP CAME TO TOWN

We prowled London streets in heels and wigs.
Beneath an orange balloon baby, we posed,
on fleek behind Josh's splayed legs.

The crowds were amazed. Dump Trump!
Don't grab pussy with blood on your hands!
Resist! Black Lives Matter! We were walking slogans,

drenched in rainbows. Trump Jr shared our photo.
We went viral, as depraved, outspoken, oversexualised –
the picture of deviancy despite my ballroom gown

of flowers. Venue Vienna a sight in purple.
Cherry very bold beside me. And let's not forget
our Family Gorgeous: Cheddar, Anna Phylactic,

Liquorice Black, garbed in the news. Chedz, Napoleonic.
Anna, a statue of life, love and liberty. Lil' Licky
with spiked hair in monochrome. I got all my sisters with me,

and our suitors behind us. The day was bright neon,
juiced up. I felt alive. Together, we told the world,
Britain is vibrant. Britain is beautiful. Britain is queer.

We don't condone dickhead plutarchs smashing
our countries to bits. Countries built on the backs
of our grandparents. Countries borne of freedom

and creativity (allegedly). Despite the heat,
the air was joyous and the camaraderie sweet,
even as I wept in front of the camera, explaining how

the local election my mum had fought for nearly
three decades turned racist again because
of the Trumps and Farrages of the world.

We stood there, chins high, legs wide, a throng
of women and crips and queers at our heels,
to remind them that we exist and we are watching.

OSIRIS

Dismembered, your fragments bound in muslin were buried
in far-flung colonial corners. Husband, I start

with your heart, interred like a dark amber fist, clenched
at the crossroads, to hold you at the crux of the matter. Your hands

I find coffined under the raven jaw of Paris's finest grand piano, fingers
tightrope-walking over strings. Your feet turn up on a beach in Bangor,

flexing like black crabs in the sand, begging for ice cream. Your head,
I find bobbing down the Blue Nile with slices of lemon, carried

miles in water jugs and tossed over Victoria Falls. Your limbs grow like trees
in logging jungles, and your shoulders are a doorframe of mahogany.

But when I piece you together, and breathe new life into your remains,
the only piece missing, I miss the most: your lifeless, withered phallus.

AFTERLIFE @ AFTERSHOCK

Pass the dry-ice strobe-stare of
the three-headed bouncer, pass
the hellhound with six black shoulders.
Descend with me into a bruise-lit underworld.
Anna Phylactic, our Queen Ishtar, rules
with eye-patch, hoop-skirt, wig.
Cyclopean giver of asphodel foams
at his grinning mouth, collects payment from
all to lift them, high spirits, to heaven;
and the DJ, hand cutting tunes like
a scythe, ferries us to the shore of the next
blue dawn. Bass rumbles, the displeasure
of life against ecstasy; then the drop comes
and we're wing-swept to rapture as one.

BOY-MACHINE

i.

Last night I dreamed of Icarus
stitching wings of silk and feather
and wax. He stretched the thatch
over a lightweight wooden frame,
the way a lover's embrace covers
a starved man with flesh. Last night
I fevered with thoughts of him.
I could taste the cleft of his buttocks,
feel the swim of saltwater sweat
down his limbs. I flew closer.

ii.

In his workshop: Leonardo
dreams of a boy-machine lifted,
held up against the sky

to wink like chiselled flint,
a specimen jewel. Leonardo
imagines a world that moves

without hands. He thinks
of wheels that spin kingdoms.
Leonardo is in love.

iii.

I bolt the wings to my forearms –
vast blades collected from helicopters,
edging like rotary petals.

I thread wire along the length
of my veins, fire muscle
with electricity, lightning from

cumulonimbus gods. I am a spark
ready to fly. I climb onto
the cottage roof, wings aimed

like a weather vane; stare
at the rushing distances of
twilight, and take off, scissor-bird,

rocket man, missile, launched
for space, through pewter skies.
I score the clouds, without weight.

BUZZING AFFY

A translation of Sappho's 'A Hymn to Aphrodite'

i.

Sister, on your precious throne of metal bling,
funking daughter of jagged skies and lightning,
domme of odes, listen close now, come on. Sister,
      I'm woman calling.

Listen how you listen, catch my morning buzz,
my voice carried over wire and horizon,
just come, as you came before. Sister, leave your
      strobe-light happening.

ii.

Your arrival is the tide-ripple of doves,
ecstasy's muscle-rhythm through the club.
You lift high over skies, glow stick bright, throw down
      heavens to hip-wind.

The haters still come. And you – my avatar,
cover girl, superstar – wait while I sulk! Quick,
blow kisses when you text back. Spit me a rap, girl,
      I need your reply.

iii.

You will say: *Who has dissed you this time, sister?*
Who stole your pissed-off heart? Can you take it back?
They'll soon give all that you gave, then give you more.
      They always return.

Tell me who to petition, who to burn out,
who to placard – you promised me this, sister.
Come now. Keep your vow. This world could soon be ours.
        Be my damn lover.

AN EXCERPT FROM 'GENESIS', THE NEW POLARI BIBLE

i.

And Gloria cackled, Let there be sparkle,
and there was sparkle.

Vada the sparkle, and vada the asterisk cascade
that glitters through the munge and banishes the naff.

Troll with me, let's vada the eek of the aquas
as they ripple and shimmer beneath the celebs.

Can you screech that it be fabulosa?
Can you vada that it be bona?

Can you troll with me, as we vada
the glamour of the sparkling munge?

ii.

Let me fashion an omie
the likes of which she ain't never espied.

She will be fierce and Mary,
with a basket to feed five grand.

Let's break her eucharist
and enjoy the nose of her bouquet.

She will be fierce, I cackle,
and she will come to slay.

MARY

Forget stars, spoiling the night with septic limelight. This time
I'll rely on a real man – not some patriarch who sends a sterile
angel in scrubs, carrying a turkey baster to impress me with His seed.
I only knew Him as dove-white Spirit brought like a shooter
in a divine vessel. Next time I want out of the public eye.
Let my child be down-to-earth, not sent sky-high. Give her kisses,
not thorns and nails. If He tries filling me with promises and lies,
or any more of His Holy Kids, I'll remind him: it's my choice.
I'll tell him it really is bad form to knock me up and ruin my figure,
without consent or even dinner. At least Zeus showered girls
with gold, and gave them sons to hold planets on their shoulders.
No, not again. Not this house. Not me. Next time, try Madonna.

A CACKLE ON THE MUCCHIO

1. And vadaing the punters, she straddled the mucchio: and when she was prompt, her omies trolled unto her,

2. And she opened her screech, and glimmed them, cackling:

3. Fabed are the nanti dinarly in fairy: for theirs is the reame of the twinkling fakement.

4. Fabed are the parniers: for they shall be parkered.

5. Fabed are the camp: for they shall garry the sod.

6. Fabed are they which do charper after bonaness: for they shall jarry the pannan.

7. Fabed are the gracies: for they shall obtain grazia.

8. Fabed are the filly of thumping cheat: for they shall vada Gloria.

9. Fabed are those who charper nanti barneys: for they shall be lubed the chavvies of the Gaylord.

10. Fabed are they which are chivvied for fabulosa's amor: for theirs is the reame of the twinkling fakement.

11. Fabed are you, when omies shall read you, and chivvy you, and shall cackle all manner of amusing nana against you, for my amor.

12. So have a kiki, and be fabulosa: for dowry is your package in the reame of the twinkling fakement: for they already have bashed the queens who came before.

13. And here finishes this throbbing screech. Troll in chillout. Kisses, duckies. Kisses.

LIKE THIS (POLARI VERSION)

A translation of Rumi

If an omi pookers you
how the sharp pagament
of all our charvering thirst
will ochy, sally your ecaf
and screech,

'Like this.'

When some cove zitarries
the boldness of the nochy fakement,
clamber with camp
on the roof and hoof
and screech,

'Like this.'

If a sister wants to clock
what fairy is,
or what Gloria's bona ink means,
lean your noggin toward her.
Keep your mush ajax.

Like this.

When some dish cackles the purano
poetry about shrouds
unvasting the lune,
loosen grop by grop the cords
of your robe.

Like this.

If any soap chidders how
Jesse Herself raised
the brown bread,
don't try to explain the kushti.
Kiss me on the oven instead.

Like this. Like this.

When trade pookers what it means
to 'gag for amour', point here.
If she pookers for my height, frown,
and with luppers gauge the space
between the grinzers on your brow.

This tall.

The fairy sometimes leaves
the bod while coming up.
When a gurrl can't imagine
or vada such suchness,
mince back into my latty.

Like this.

When bones moan
to each other in the cottage
cloister, deep in harva,
they're jibbing
our story.

Like this.

I am a volta where fairies live.
Vada into this
deepening azure,
while the becker breathes
the patter flash.

Like this.

When an omie palone
pookers what
there is to do,
sindarry the randall
in his lills.

Like this. Like this.

When she 'arry varries
back from Cruz,
she'll poke just her cap
around the rim
of the jin to shake us

like this.

THE KISS

We kiss in front of your monument,
our lips pressed like this, the ovals
of mouths bunched into fists.

We hold tight with soft arms,
and tango in rows, our bodies
all faces and hooked elbows.

We kiss outside parliament
to show you we're here. We kiss
in the street. We kiss without fear.

THE MARRIAGE

In the shade we fold into bows of limbs,
our shadows pool among roots. You succumb,
pull from the branch low-slung bulbs of delight.
Your knife orbits the golden fruit, disrobes
its pithy sunlight. You give it to me:
a half-moon, a bowl of amethysts.
This dowry in your fist illuminates;
the canopy of the blossoming tree
becomes sanctuary no more, reveals
flesh in dark ridges, wet, scattered with seeds.
I am anointed with juice that beads and runs free.
You feed me morsels like purple stars. Fill
the groove of my collarbone. You dress me in
this sap necklace. Make me your shining queen.

HONEYBEE

Scooped honey pours from your fingers,
gold jelly cascades over nacre.

You smear it around my anus,
and even inside, before you

drag me into Sackville Gardens.
I hear the bees fire the sky like

Zeppelins, their aim snipering my
parted thighs, that rosy silken skin.

THE WAYS I MIGHT LOVE YOU, GIVEN THE CHANCE

1.
I might cuddle you on cold mornings,
both of us bound in flannel dressing gowns,
sipping mugs of hot chocolate
with a cat sliding itself between our limbs.

2.
I might be so shocked at your touch,
electrified to a fossil,
that I merely stand, an adoring statue
while the fridge door hangs open.

3.
I might bed you in reams of poetry
dedicated to your eyes, your lips,
your toenails, your verrucas,
while you gradually suffocate.

4.
I might cook your dinner
and never work again,
as you go out and bring home
the rindless back bacon.

5.
I might brandish a whip,
chain you to the bed,
as I make impassioned demands
you can never meet.

6.
But I might just be me
loving you,
with the bills and the shopping
and sod-all on TV.

LIKE THIS

A remix of Rumi
for Stefan

If anyone asks you what satisfaction looks like,
smile, lift your face and say, 'Like this.'
When a friend remarks on the grace of night sky,
climb on the roof, and dance like this.
If anyone wants to know your soul, lean your head
toward them. Hold your face close. Like this.
When a child marvels at the first glimpse of full moon,
unknot the day's thoughts. Sigh. Like this.
If anyone wonders how God raised the dead,
don't try to explain. Kiss me on the lips. Like this. Like this.
When someone asks what it means to 'die for love',
ask them what it means to 'live for love' instead. Like this.
When someone asks what there is to do, light the candle in hand.
When lovers moan, they're telling our story. Like this.
When you come home, you put your head around
the door frame to surprise me. Like this.
When you feel blind and lost, look up.
A little wind cleans the eye. Like this.

VADA THAT – GLOSSARY

Aunt nell – ear, listen (also: nellyarda)

Patter flash – gossip, chat, ostentatious or pretentious speech

Gardy loo – 'Look out!'

Troll – walk, provoke (as in online)

Lallies – legs

The Dilly – Piccadilly (London, but perhaps also Manchester), a high street or similar

Brandy – bottom (from Cockney rhyming slang: 'brandy and rum')

Brandy latch – toilet

Vada – see, spy, look

Dolly – pretty

Trade, trick – a sexual partner, though only a 'trick' need always be a 'john'

Reef – to feel, to grope (especially the bulge or crotch)

Harva – anal sex

Omi – man

Scotches – legs

Thews – thighs, sinews

Charpering – finding

Vera – gin

Nochy – night

Journo – day

Laus – chases

Munge – darkness

Sharda – though

Affaire – a lover, a serious partner as opposed to a fling

Pogey – money

Head – bed

Back slum – public lavatory

Meat rack – brothel, a parade of rent boys lined up for punters

Charpering carsey – police cell

Auntie – older gay man, role model

Mama – mentor

The bones – a boyfriend or husband

Eek – face

Bona – good

RUMI GLOSSARY

'arry varry (Harry varry) – arrive (backformation from Italian: arrivare)

Becker – wind (from Romany)

Brown bread – dead

Cap – head

Cheuri – tongue, speech

Chidder – wonder (backformation from Italian: chiedersi)

Fairy – soul or spirit

Grinzer – wrinkle (backformation from Italian: grinza)

Grop – knot

Hoof – dance

Ink – stink, smell (from Cockney rhyming slang: pen and ink)

Jin – door

Jinny, jinnik – to know

Lills – hands

Mumper – candle (from Romany)

Ochy – look (backformation from Italian: occhiata)

Oven – mouth

Pagament – satisfaction (backformation from Italian: appagamento)

Pooker – to speak or ask (from Romani: 'pooker', which means Romani slang itself)

Randall – candle (from Cockney rhyming slang: Harry Randall)

Sally – rise, ascend, lift (backformation from Italian: salire)

Shroud – cloud (from Cockney rhyming slang: Turin shroud)

Sindarry – to light, kindle, switch on (backformation from Italian: 'accendare')

soap – dope (from Cockney rhyming slang: Joe Soap)

Squash – wash (from Cockney rhyming slang: Bob Squash)Vast – covered

Venny – come out

Vochy – voice, speak

Yews – eyes

Zitarry – mention

ABOUT THE AUTHOR

Adam Lowe is a writer, performer and publisher from Leeds, UK, though he currently lives in Manchester. He is the UK's LGBT+ History Month Poet Laureate and was Yorkshire's Poet for 2012 . He writes poetry, plays and fiction, and he occasionally performs in drag as Beyonce Holes. He is of mixed Caribbean (St. Kitts), British and Irish descent. He graduated with both a BA and MA from the University of Leeds.

He writes about disability, LGBT+ experiences and the lives of mixed-race Black British communities. Carol Rumens of *The Guardian* describes him as a 'versatile and widely published young writer'.

He founded and runs Young Enigma, a writer development project for young writers; is Editor-in-Chief of *Vada Magazine* and Dog Horn Publishing; and is Publicity Officer for Peepal Tree Press. He has performed around the world, at festivals and conferences, including the Black and Asian Writers Conference. He is an advocate for LGBT+ rights and sits on the management committee for Schools OUT UK, the charity that founded LGBT History Month in the UK.

In 2013, he was announced as one of 10 Black and Asian 'advanced poets' for The Complete Works II (founded by Bernardine Evaristo) with Mona Arshi, Jay Bernard, Kayo Chingoni, Rishi Dastidar, Edward Doegar, Inua Ellams, Sarah Howe, Eileen Pun and Warsan Shire, which resulted in the anthology *Ten: The New Wave*, edited by Karen McCarthy-Woolf (Bloodaxe). He was mentored on the programme by Patience Agbabi. He also made the list of '20 under 40' writers in Leeds for the LS13 Awards, where Lowe was given as an example of 'the non-conformist and boundary-breaking approach to writing in Leeds'.